LIVING WELL

EATING
FOR GOOD HEALTH

by Shirley Wimbish Gray

THE CHILD'S WORLD
CHANHASSEN, MINNESOTA

The Child's World

Published in the United States of America by The Child's World®
P.O. Box 326, Chanhassen, MN 55317-0326
800-599-READ
www.childsworld.com

Subject Consultant:
Diana Ruschhaupt,
Director of Programs,
Ruth Lilly Health
Education Center,
Indianapolis,
Indianapolis

Photo Credits: Cover: IT Stock Free/Creatas; Bettman/Corbis: 12; Bob Rowan; Progressive Image/Corbis: 17, 18, 26; Corbis: 6 (Fukuhara, Inc.), 8, 10 (Tom Stewart), 13 (Charlie Samuels), 14 (Roger Ressmeyer), 15 (Nathan Benn), 16, 19 (Bruce Burkhardt), 20 (Norbert Schaefer), 21right (Chris Collins), 22 (Ariel Skelley), 24, 25 (Roy Morsch), 27 (Ronnie Kaufman), 29 (Jon Feingersh), 31 (Tom & Dee Ann McCarthy); Custom Medical Stock Pictures: 11; Getty Images/Brand X Pictures: 9; Keith Dannemiller/Corbis Saba: 21; Photo Edit: 5 (Tony Freeman), 23 (Myrleen Ferguson Cate); U. S. Department of Agriculture: 7.

The Child's World®: Mary Berendes, Publishing Director

For Editorial Directions, Inc.: E. Russell Primm, Editorial Director; Elizabeth K. Martin, Line Editor; Katie Marsico, Assistant Editor; Olivia Nellums, Editorial Assistant; Susan Hindman, Copy Editor; Sarah E. De Capua, Proofreader; Peter Garnham and Chris Simms, Fact Checkers; Tim Griffin/IndexServ, Indexer; Elizabeth K. Martin and Matthew Messbarger, Photo Researchers and Selectors

Library of Congress Cataloging-in-Publication Data
Gray, Shirley W.
  Eating for good health / by Shirley Wimbish Gray.
      p. cm. — (Living well)
Includes index.
Contents: Healthy food helps!—What is good nutrition?—Protecting your body—Smart foods—Healthy choices.
  ISBN 1-59296-079-0 (lib. bdg. : alk. paper)
  1. Nutrition—Juvenile literature. 2. Children—Nutrition—Juvenile literature.
[1. Nutrition. 2. Food habits.] I. Title. II. Series: Living well (Child's World (Firm)
  RA784.G727 200
  613.2—dc21   2003006277

TABLE OF CONTENTS

CHAPTER ONE

HEALTHY
FOOD HELPS!

Jeffrey plays for his school football team, the Panthers. Before

their first game, Jeffrey and his teammates had lunch together.

They ate turkey sandwiches and fruit. Everyone drank several

glasses of water. "No soft drinks and no chips today," the coach

told the team. "I want your bodies to have the right fuel for the

game tonight."

That night, Jeffrey made an important play. He saw a player

from the other team running with the ball. Jeffrey ran as fast as

he could and tackled the player. The other player did not score.

Jeffrey's lunch gave him the energy he needed to run fast.

You know that your body uses food as fuel. But did you

know that your body needs certain types of food every day? And that it needs the right amount each day? Learning about nutrition

(noo-TRISH-un) will help you make good choices about what you

eat. Then your body will have what it needs, just like Jeffrey's did.

Eating well before the game helped Jeremy make an important play.

CHAPTER TWO

WHAT IS
GOOD NUTRITION?

Good nutrition means eating the right types and amounts of food.

The body uses **nutrients** from food as building blocks. For

example, it uses calcium (KAL-see-um) to build bones and teeth.

Calcium is found mainly in milk and other dairy foods. Without

enough of these foods, bones would be weak and would break easily.

So how do you know what kinds of food to eat and how much

Dairy products such as these are rich in calcium and help make our bones and teeth stronger.

you need each day? One way is to use the Food Guide Pyramid. It divides the food we eat into five main groups. The foods we should eat the most of come from the bottom of the pyramid. We only need a small amount of the foods at the top.

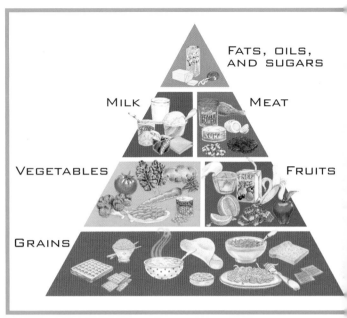

A nutritious diet is composed of eating the right amounts of different kinds of foods from the Food Guide Pyramid.

At the bottom of the pyramid are foods made from grains. These include bread, cereal, rice, and pasta. These foods give your body energy.

Just on top of that group are the fruit and vegetable groups. These foods contain **vitamins** that our bodies need. Did you know that eating carrots helps you see better in the dark? Fruits and vegetables also help prevent diseases.

Next in the pyramid are the milk and meat groups. These foods come mainly from animals such as fish, chicken, and cattle. Foods in these groups contain calcium and protein (PRO-teen). Your body uses protein to make muscles.

Children and teenagers need more calcium each day than

Hamburgers are not only a tasty treat, they are high in protein as well.

adults do. Drinking milk is one of the easiest ways to get calcium. You can also eat cheese and yogurt.

This delicious salad might be a normal lunch for a vegetarian.

Some people do not want to eat protein that comes from animals. They are called vegetarians (vej-uh-TER-ee-uhnz). Vegetarians can get their protein from plant sources, such as nuts and beans.

At the top of the pyramid are foods made from fats, oils, and sugars. Candy bars and cookies are examples of this group. Our bodies need very few of these foods each day.

A Colorful Plate

Need an easy way to know if you are making healthy food choices? Let color be your guide. Most foods that contain vitamins and minerals are colored. Colored fruits and vegetables can also help prevent diseases. Orange foods, such as carrots and squash, keep your eyes healthy. Red foods, such as tomatoes and watermelons, may help prevent some kinds of cancer. So, the more colorful your plate, the more healthy your choices. Try a fruit salad—purple grapes, red apples, yellow bananas, and oranges. Or make a soup—red tomatoes, green beans, orange carrots, and yellow squash. You can add color to your breakfast with blueberries and red strawberries. At dinner, you could make a green salad with yellow and red pepper slices for your family!

Another part of good nutrition is giving our bodies plenty of water. Most of us need at least six glasses of water every day. You will need more than that when it is hot or when you exercise. It is a good idea to carry a plastic bottle of water with you when you go outside to play.

CHAPTER THREE

How Does Eating Well Keep You Healthy?

For a long time, doctors thought that germs caused all diseases. They did not know that people could get sick from not eating the right kinds of foods.

For example, scurvy is a disease that sailors used to get hundreds of years ago. In 1747, a ship left England for Massachusetts Colony in America. While at sea, the ship's crew became ill with scurvy. The

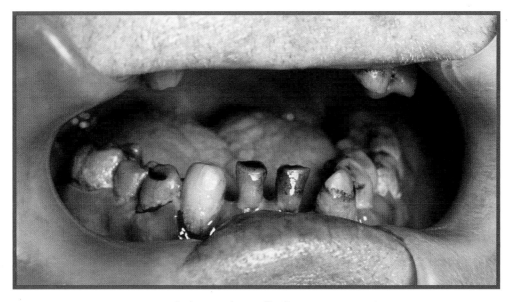

Sailors used to suffer from scurvy,
a disease that caused problems with their gums and teeth.

An engraving of James Lind giving citrus fruits to sailors with scurvy.

doctor on the ship tried different ways to help the men get well. He

told some of them to swallow spoonfuls of vinegar each day. He told

others to drink seawater.

One group of sailors ate oranges and limes. They were the only

men who got well. From then on, British ships carried limes for the

sailors to eat on long trips. Eating the fruit kept the sailors from

getting scurvy.

It was not until the early 1900s that scientists began talking about

vitamins. *Vita* means "needed for life" in Latin. Oranges and limes have Vitamin C in them. Now we know that our bodies need Vitamin

C to prevent scurvy and other diseases.

Few people in the United States get scurvy anymore. But Americans are developing other health problems because of the foods they eat. One of the major problems is **obesity.** Today, one out of five children is overweight. This is a new health problem. Twenty years ago, fewer children were overweight.

Many children become overweight because of poor eating habits. They eat too many foods from the top of the Food Group Pyramid, such as candy and chips. They also may not get enough exercise. Sitting in front of the TV

Poor eating habits, such as eating too much junk food, can cause obesity.

Flying a kite is one way to exercise and have fun, instead of watching TV.

while eating a bag of chips after school is not a healthy habit. Eating

an apple and playing kickball with friends is a better idea. Turning on

music and dancing with your friends is a smart idea, too.

Teachers know that good nutrition makes a difference at school.

Children who do not eat right receive lower grades. They also get sick

more often and miss school. They may not have enough energy to

run on the playground. Your teacher can help you learn more about

making good choices about the food you eat.

CHAPTER FOUR

What Vitamins Does Your Body Need?

People who study how the body uses food are called nutritionists (noo-TRISH-uh-nists) or dieticians (dye-uh-TISH-uns). They often work in schools or hospitals. They may also work for companies that get food ready so it can be sold in grocery stores.

Nutritionists study which foods are the best for us to eat.

Fruits and vegetables are great sources of vitamins and minerals.

The person in charge of your school's lunchroom is probably a nutritionist. Nutritionists have discovered 13 vitamins that our bodies need. Vitamin D is the only one that our bodies can make. We have to get the rest of them from the food we eat.

Vitamins are not the only things the body needs to get from foods. Your body also needs small amounts of **minerals.** For example, the body needs tiny amounts of iodine. People who do

Whole wheat bread has more nutrients than plain white bread.

not get enough of this mineral may suffer from a disease called

goiter. Eating tuna and other kinds of fish can help you get

enough iodine. Calcium is another mineral that our bodies need.

We should be able to get vitamins and minerals from the

different foods we eat. But that isn't always the case. Sometimes,

getting food ready to sell in stores makes it less healthy. When food

companies strip off the brown shell surrounding these two grains, the result is white rice and white flour. These are not as healthy as

the whole grain rice or flour. This is because the brown shell

contains vitamins, fiber, minerals, protein, and carbohydrates.

Vitamins and minerals can be added to food products to make

them healthier. The vitamin thiamin is added to rice and bread.

Vitamin D is added to

most cartons of milk.

Iodine is added to salt.

This does not change the

taste of the food. It just

helps people get the

nutrients they need.

Sometimes people take

pills to make sure they are

Vitamin D is added to milk to make it healthier.

getting enough vitamins and minerals. But you will not need to do this if you get those nutrients from your food. Be sure to eat different types of foods to get the many vitamins and minerals you need. Eating at least five servings of fruits and vegetables every day also helps.

The Sunshine Vitamin

Vitamin D is called the sunshine vitamin because the human body can make it with the help of the sun! The sun's rays trigger the skin to start making Vitamin D. Vitamin D helps the body use calcium to build strong bones. Children who do not get enough of it may develop a disease called rickets.

Rickets can be a problem for some children who live in northern climates. The rays of the sun are not very strong in these climates during the winter. This means that people who live there cannot make the Vitamin D their bodies need. They have to get it from the foods they eat. Vitamin D is found naturally in a few foods, such as codfish and salmon. It is also added to most cow's milk.

CHAPTER FIVE

ARE YOU MAKING
HEALTHY FOOD CHOICES?

Every day, you make choices about the types of food you eat. You also make choices about how much to eat. There are easy ways that you can make these healthy choices.

You can make healthy food choices, such as being sure to eat lots of vegetables.

Pay attention to the serving size of what you eat. Instead of a big bag of popcorn, choose a handful of jelly beans!

One thing to think about is serving size. Maybe you want some candy when you go to the movies with your friends. Candy is at the top of the food pyramid, so you know you should not eat much of it. Choose a small candy bar instead of a large one. Or choose to share the large bar with several friends.

You can make healthy food choices even when you are eating fast food.

Think about size when you go to a fast-food restaurant, too. The menu might offer super-size servings of fries and soft drinks. Most people do not need the extra fat and sugar in the large servings.

A small bag of fries or a small cola is the best choice. A salad with your hamburger is an even better choice!

Variety is important in healthy eating, too. Choose different foods within each group. Don't eat only apples from the fruit group. Try oranges and berries sometimes, too! When choosing

You may love apples,
but try some other fruits and vegetables, too.

your meals, think about how many of the food groups your choices

include. A sandwich made of turkey, lettuce, tomatoes, and a slice

of cheese between two slices of bread has food from four groups.

A peanut butter sandwich includes only two food groups.

Try to include several food groups in your meals. It's easy to do this with a sandwich.

Do you have a snack when you get home from school? That is another chance for you to make a good choice about the food you eat. Choose foods from the bottom

An after-school snack of carrots and celery is the perfect study food!

or middle of the food pyramid instead of the top. Low-fat cheese and crackers make a good snack. So does celery stuffed with peanut butter. Some children like to mix fruit and cottage cheese together for a snack.

You can even make a healthy choice if you buy food from a snack machine. Animal crackers or pretzels are good choices. They do not have much fat or sugar in them. If you are not allergic to them, a package of peanuts is better than a candy bar.

Have you heard of a drink machine that sells milk instead of soft drinks? Many schools in New York, Wisconsin, and other states have this type of machine. The milk comes in several flavors, such as chocolate, cookies and cream, and caramel! Some schools

There are lots of different flavors of milk. Chocolate milk is one of the tastiest!

Healthy food choices will keep you healthy throughout your life.

put the milk machines near the gym or in the hall. Then students

can choose a healthy drink whenever they are thirsty. What good

food choices have you made today?

Glossary

goiter (GOY-ter) A goiter is a disease of the thyroid gland in the front of the neck.

minerals (MIN-ur-uhlz) Minerals are elements found in the ground that cannot be made by living things. Certain minerals are important for good health.

nutrients (NOO-tree-uhnts) Nutrients are found in foods and are needed to live and stay healthy.

obesity (oh-BEE-si-tee) Obesity is a condition where the body contains too much fat.

vitamins (VYE-tuh-minz) Vitamins are made by living things. The body needs to get them from food to work properly.

Questions and Answers about Nutrition

How much milk should I drink every day? Children ages 4 to 8 need three glasses of milk a day. Children between the ages of 9 and 18 need four glasses a day.

How do I know what types of nutrients are in the food I buy at the store? Read the nutrition fact label on the package. It lists the amounts of vitamins, minerals, sugar, fat, and protein in a food or drink. The label will show a percentage, written as %DV or % Daily Value. In a serving of food, 5% DV or less of a nutrient is low, and 20% DV or more is high.

I want to be good at soccer. Should I eat a special diet? The best way to be good at soccer or any other sport is to practice often and eat right. Be sure to follow the Food Guide Pyramid. Young athletes need several different types of foods to play well.

Did You Know?

▸ Only 2 percent of children meet the daily Food Guide Pyramid recommendations.

▸ The average American child spends about 24 hours each week watching television. This is time that could be spent playing and getting exercise.

▸ In the United States, one out of every five children is overweight.

▸ Babies are born with more than 300 bones. As they grow up, some of the bones grow together. Adults only have 206 bones. Each one is made of calcium.

▸ Poor dietary choices and lack of physical activity account for more than 300,000 deaths in the United States each year.

A poor diet and not enough exercise is a bad combination. Remember that all the time you spend watching TV, you could be playing with your friends.

How to Learn More about Nutrition

At the Library

Haduch, Bill, and Rick Stromoski (illustrator). *Food Rules!: The Stuff You Munch, Its Crunch, Its Punch, and Why You Sometimes Lose Your Lunch.* New York: Dutton Children's Books, 2001.

Rockwell, Lizzy. *Good Enough to Eat: A Kid's Guide to Food and Nutrition.* New York: HarperCollins Publishers, 1999.

Sears, William, Martha Sears, and Christie Watts Kelly. *Eat Healthy, Feel Great: A Kid's Guide to Nutrition.* Boston: Little, Brown, 2002.

On the Web

Visit our home page for lots of links about healthy eating:
http://www.childsworld.com/links.html

Note to Parents, Teachers, and Librarians: We routinely verify our Web links to make sure they're safe, active sites—so encourage your readers to check them out!

Through the Mail or by Phone

American Dietetic Association
120 South Riverside Plaza, Suite 2000
Chicago, IL 60606-6995
312/899-0040

American School Food Service Association (ASFSA)
700 South Washington Street
Suite 300
Alexandria, VA 22314
703/739-3900

Center for Nutrition Policy and Promotion
3101 Park Center Drive, Room 1034
Alexandria, VA 22302-1594
703/305-7600

You can stay healthy by eating foods that are good for you.

Index

About the Author

Shirley Wimbish Gray has been a writer and educator for more than 25 years and has published more than a dozen nonfiction books for children. She also coordinates cancer education programs at the University of Arkansas for Medical Sciences and consults as a writer with scientists and physicians. She lives with her husband and two sons in Little Rock, Arkansas.